3/4 Full is a cup tha
caresses the heart, inf
Nathan is gone ten y
pact in a pond, his life ripples outward forever.

  ~ Mitchell Chefitz, author of
    The Curse of Blessings

*It takes a powerfully steady heart and mind to embrace the
immense joy and profound suffering that life brings.*

    *Peggy Gaines demonstrates how meditation can help us
achieve equanimity and the freedom to love what is, life as it is.*

    *A transforming read for anyone but I especially recom-
mend it for those determined not to allow suffering to eclipse
the love and joy in their lives.*

  ~ Peggy Rios, PhD, Program Director Cancer Support
    Community Greater Miami

*This poignant and moving book is a testimony to the human
spirit and coping with a unimaginable tragedy. There are
lessons detailed which can help any person or family facing
such a sad and overwhelming challenge and indeed show the
true power of hope.*

  ~ Henry S Friedman, MD
    Deputy Director
    Preston Robert Tisch Brain Tumor Center
    at Duke Medical Center

An amazingly positive perspective of life with a technique explaining how to acquire it. I enjoyed every chapter.

~ Doured Daghistani, MD Pediatric Hematology and Oncology, Miami, FL

This book is an example for all of us on how to address end-of-life issues with our loved ones!

~ Gary X Lancelotta, Ph.D., ABPP Director, Child Psychology Associates, Miami, FL

3/4 FULL

Blessings From a New Perspective

PEGGY GAINES

Photos by Jeff Aresty

ISBN-10: 0-9975762-4-3
ISBN-13: 978-0-9975762-4-5

This book is dedicated to my family who has given me so much.
For the support and encouragement of my husband Michael,
the love and friendship of my daughter Heather,
and for the soul lessons of my son Nathan,
I have been truly blessed.

CHAPTER 1

You can argue with the way things are.
You'll lose, but only 100% of the time.
~ Byron Katie

"This is where God lives," I exclaimed as we looked over the beautiful mountain lake surrounded by pine trees. We had hiked all morning ready for an adventure. Coming from sea level Miami, the climb winded but invigorated us. My two teenage kids, Nathan 17 and Heather 14 led the way, making noise as we climbed to prevent us from surprising bears that inhabited Glacier National Park, Montana. We collapsed on a boulder and admired the view. Big chunks of ice and snow sat like icebergs in the lake, surrounded by massive mountains. The air was pristine, crisp and clear; the sky a brilliant blue. The setting was breath-taking, surely heaven couldn't be more beautiful. The kids seemed to agree with my assessment. We quietly ate our lunch as the bright sun warmed us and then rested under the pine trees looking up at the sky.

"Smell the air, it's so clean and fresh! Look at the way the sun shines through the branches. Isn't beautiful? Keep this memory tucked away in the recesses of your mind. You may need to remember it someday when you're writing a paper or maybe when you're sick and lying in bed." Little did I know how prophetic that motherly advice would be.

The air was getting cooler as the sun began its descent behind the mountains. We packed up and began our return, admiring the bear grass that has a massive explosion every 7 years. How lucky we were to witness its prolific beauty. Tall lacy flowers known as bear grass filled the valleys. These are a favorite snack of the bears, both brown and black, that call this park home. We could tell bears had passed through, as the heads of bear grass were snapped off, a telltale sign that someone had enjoyed an afternoon nibble. We traveled further down the path and suddenly in the distance about 50 yards ahead we saw a mother and her cub. The mother was the size of a Volkswagen bus and her cub a Mini-Cooper. It was thrilling to see them but we stayed upwind and respectfully waited until they had crossed the path and ambled on down the mountain. This was their home and they certainly had the right of way.

Later that evening as we recovered from our hike, Nathan began a postcard to his girlfriend. Nathan was a typical teenage boy. He was tall, about 6 foot 4 with dark thick hair. He was smart, funny and kind. Since 6th grade, he had one or another girlfriend, and now he was writing to his current one. Nathan had begun working out at the gym about two or three years before and was always lifting more weight than he should. As he began his note, he told his sister that he was hav-

Nathan. He's seated on a boulder in Glacier National Park with Many Glacier Hotel in the background.

ing a hard time writing. When I heard about it, I thought he had probably just pinched a nerve from lifting weight incorrectly. His dad was a bit of a hypochondriac and I thought he had inherited the trait. I reassured him that if he was still having problems when we returned we would find a chiropractor to help him.

As our vacation progressed, Nathan came to me and said he was having trouble saying words. I didn't hear a thing and dismissed his concern. "Everyone trips over words once in a while," I told him, again thinking he was having a little male anxiety for no real reason. The trip was filled with fun; more hiking plus an eight-hour horseback ride through the mountains and a day of white water rafting. I love the outdoors and our vacations were always filled with hiking, canoeing and cycling plus even a little camping. I wanted our children to love the outdoors as much as I did and our hike to Iceberg Lake was a trip we would never forget.

* * *

Lesson One: The beauty of nature is nourishment for the soul. It strengthens the spirit and creates a communion with God.

CHAPTER 2

Your children are not your children. They are the sons and daughters of Life's longing for itself. They came through you but not from you and though they are with you yet they belong not to you.

~ Kahlil Gibran

As I held Nathan, only 6 days old, I thought I had never seen a more beautiful baby. I was a labor and delivery nurse and had seen my share of newborns. All babies were cute, but my baby was amazing; or so I thought. Just like every new mother I couldn't believe how precious this little one was. My husband Michael is Jewish, and I had been raised Catholic. Somehow this seemed to create a problem for the respective religions. Each religion wanted us to promise that we would raise our child solely according to their set beliefs. I wasn't about to give up my Christian beliefs and I would never ask Mike to give up his. I found it hard to believe that God actually cares about all the man-made rules that cause so much division in our world. I felt God's vision was much bigger than that and not restricted to rules and regulations.

We were in agreement that we would do it our own way. We would have both a Bris and a Baptism. We created our own ceremony and Mike assumed the role of the rabbi and read from the Jewish text. I read a favorite selection by Kahlil Gibran, reminding parents that the child does not come from you, he comes through you. We covered all the bases; Nathan was baptized and had a bris. If this child couldn't get into heaven, no one could.

I was standing in the room at the hospital ready to begin the ceremony when suddenly I started crying.

"What's wrong?" Mike asked.

"Nothing," I replied, "I guess I'm just a little tired and emotional." What I didn't want to share was a message that I somehow heard just at that moment.

"This child will not be yours for long" was the message I received. I filed this ominous premonition away. As the years passed, I didn't focus on it but I also didn't forget it.

We had been home from our vacation in Montana about 10 days when Nathan came into my bedroom. I was busy cleaning out a closet and piles of clothing were strewn about the bed and floor.

"Mom!" Nathan insisted. "Mom! Look at me, look at my smile!" I was busy folding and sorting and didn't respond immediately. "Mom!" Nathan called again, "Look at my smile and then look at my driver's license," he demanded.

I looked at his smile; it was crooked. That did seem a little odd and then I looked at his driver's license, where his smile was perfectly symmetrical. As a nurse I remembered the sage advice of an older mentor, "Always assume the least dramatic reason for a problem and you'll probably be right. Never assume the worst."

Have you ever had an experience where the bottom seemed to drop out of your life? Has something happened that completely caught you off guard?

Maybe you went into work at the job you thought would be yours until retirement and suddenly you learn that your position has been eliminated.

Or maybe the person you thought you were going to spend the rest of your life with for better or for worse, until death do you part walks in and says "I don't think I can do this anymore."

Or maybe you go into the doctor's for a routine checkup and you're told, "We need to do some more tests because there's something that's a little questionable."

Or maybe you made some investments that you were sure were going to set you up financially for life and suddenly the market drops and you lose everything.

I had one of those days; one of those days that was a seminal event that changed everything. One of those days that will forever be a marker in my life. One of those days that delineates life as it existed before and life as it existed after.

This was one of those days.

Looking at my son, I tried to imagine the cause of his crooked smile. "Surely it wasn't a stroke," I thought. It could be Bells Palsy or perhaps it was a pinched nerve, my earlier thought. Perhaps he had pinched a nerve lifting weights and that affected his hand and also affected his smile. It seemed like a stretch but I hoped it was something fixable like that.

In the back of my mind, another possibility inexplicably came to the surface. "Brain tumor," I thought. Surely it wasn't that. I would never say such a thing out loud.

Incredibly, immediately after that possibility crossed my mind, Nathan looked at me and said, "I think I have a brain tumor."

Suddenly, the morning of his Bris/Baptism, almost 18 years earlier, came rushing back to me. "This is what that message meant," I thought. Hopefully, I would be wrong.

Of course it was Friday afternoon. Do children ever get sick at any other time? I called Nathan's doctor, spoke to the nurse and was able to get in for the last appointment of the day.

The physician did an exam and then with the same nonchalant tone that one would deliver the diagnosis of a cold or strep throat, said, "I think he may have a brain tumor." I started to cry and he admonished me, "You are a nurse, surely you must have suspected that."

* * *

Lesson Two: Be mindful of the way you speak. You may just be stating the facts but the words you say can hit a person at a visceral level.

CHAPTER 3

We must let go of the life we have planned so as to accept the one that's waiting for us.
~ Joseph Campbell

The truth is, both Nathan and I had suspected a brain tumor, but I'm not really sure why. Nathan hadn't had any of the typical symptoms that are normally associated with a brain tumor; no headaches, no seizures, just the difficulty writing, his awareness of trouble pronouncing words (which still wasn't apparent to me) and now the crooked smile. I had liked this physician up to this point but his curt retort made me reassess my approval rating. Although I felt his admonishment was unsympathetic, I also wondered if it was actually due to the fact that he was uncomfortable with the possible prognosis for this intelligent young man, who was ready to begin his senior year in high school in a matter of weeks.

We had a CAT scan scheduled for the next morning and somehow my sweet husband pulled some strings and got an appointment Monday morning with the chief neurosurgeon at the hospital on his first day back from vacation. It was honestly miraculous that we were able to get in to see him so quickly.

The tests showed Nathan had a 4 cm, malignant brain tumor. It was about the size of a lemon. If you are a parent, you know there is little worse in life than finding out that your child is facing a life-threatening illness.

The demands of motherhood were ramping up to levels I had never anticipated. My husband worked to find the most promising treatment, the top hospitals and the best doctors, but I was on the front lines. I needed to make all the appointments, drive to all the doctors' offices and hospitals, keep track of the medications, comfort and care for my sick child, and most importantly be the head cheerleader, always keeping a positive outlook. What I really wanted to do was crawl back into bed and pull the sheets up over my head. But that was not an option. I needed something to help me cope with this terrifying situation.

Fortunately, I had what I needed, meditation. I always had a good relationship with God and I certainly leaned on Him now. But the tool that I used to augment that relationship was meditation. It gave me an inner strength that literally kept me breathing through this ordeal.

I began meditating about 6 years earlier because, like so many people, I was having trouble falling asleep. I bought a book on meditation, began listening to some cassette tapes and went to a class or two. Pretty soon I was meditating 20 minutes daily. My sleep improved dramatically and life was perfect–or at least I thought it was at the time.

With my son's diagnosis, life changed for all of us. I stopped working and focused on getting my son the help that he needed. Nathan had surgery and began treatment, which included traveling from our home in Miami to Duke Medical center in North Carolina. I meditated everywhere; in every plane, waiting room and exam room. I taught Nathan how to meditate and he did it when he was getting radiation, chemotherapy and multiple MRIs.

It was, of course, Nathan's life that changed most dramatically. When Nathan woke up in the recovery room from his first surgery, his first words were "I love life". My heart overflowed with love for him. We were beginning a journey into the unknown.

* * *

Lesson 3: As a mother, no matter what happens, when your child faces a crisis you rise to the occasion.

CHAPTER 4

Life is 10% what happens and 90% how you respond to it.

~ Charles Swindle

Nathan had anticipated an exciting senior year in high school. He had already been accepted at the University of Florida and had sent in his application for the dorm where he wanted to live. But our reality had changed. We needed to be adaptable, but we also needed to be positive and keep hope in the forefront. We needed every tool possible to help us navigate the road ahead.

Nathan had a second surgery and he had rounds and rounds of chemo and radiation and multiple MRIs. The treatment was very debilitating making it impossible for him to attend school so he completed his class requirements online. It certainly wasn't the way he had envisioned his senior year of high school.

One day we went to the oncologist for a regular checkup. By this point, Nathan had endured two brain surgeries and had a nasty looking scar on the back of his head. His thick hair was completely gone and he no longer had the physique he had worked so hard to build. His girlfriend had left him, he had lost all his hair, lost all his muscles and he walked with a limp. His body image had definitely taken a huge hit.

The doctor walked into the room and asked, "Nathan, how are you today? Is the glass half-full or half empty?"

Without missing a beat, Nathan replied, "The glass is ¾ full." I was very proud of him. I hadn't realized that response was even a possible answer.

Nathan was teaching me to keep the right perspective. He was looking at what he had and not at what he had lost.

* * *

Lesson 4: Keep perspective and look at the bigger picture. The Universe is offering us a tray full of gifts and yet we overlook them. Sometimes it is only in the darkness that we see the light.

CHAPTER 5

As soap is to the body, so laugher is to the soul.
~ A Jewish Proverb

Nathan completed his senior year requirements online and was able to walk across the stage to graduate with his high school class. He was physically weak but strong in spirit. After the commencement he went out to lunch with his friends to celebrate just like in the old days.

His college plans were adjusted. Instead of going away to school at the University of Florida he would begin college at the University of Miami in our hometown. He would live in the dorm and come home when he needed to recover from the effects of the chemo, which he was still undergoing.

Life went on with more chemo and radiation. We would fly to Duke Medical Center about every 6 weeks for a check-up and saw the oncologist in Miami who administered the prescribed treatment.

Finally, after 2-½ years of treatment the MRI showed no signs of cancer. Nathan was cancer-free! A clean bill of health! I was ecstatic but I noticed that the doctor did not display my level of enthusiasm. I noted it, but dismissed it. I wanted to focus on what we had and what we had was good!

Nathan was now in his sophomore year of college. He was feeling pretty healthy but in December I began to notice that he was having trouble walking. He acted as though he didn't notice it but he began to lean on my shoulder for support as we walked. Over a matter of weeks he became more and more unsteady on his feet. I made an appointment with the oncologist and a MRI was ordered. No new brain tumor appeared. The oncologist referred me to a neurologist who did a spinal tap among other tests. No cause could be determined for the loss of balance. As his mobility worsened, Nathan began choosing to stay at home instead of living at the dorm. I drove him to school each day and parked as close as I could to whatever building he needed to go to for his class.

One day, as I was waiting for him in the parking lot on campus, Nathan began walking from his class to the car. He lost his balance and fell onto the hot asphalt and did not have the strength to lift himself up off the pavement. My sweet son was no longer the strong young man he once had been. He lay helpless on the burning asphalt until I happened to turn around in the car and see him lying there. It broke my heart. I told him that he would have to quit attending classes until we figured out what was causing his loss of mobility.

This was a difficult time for Nathan. It was hard for him to accept that he was losing control. I suggested he begin to use a cane. He was resistant. The changes were happening incredibly quickly. Every day his ability to walk deceased more and more. By the time he agreed to use a cane it was too late. He was at the point that he needed to use a walker. This was horrifying to him. A few days passed and he came around to accepting the use of a walker but his strength had deteriorated further so that now he needed a wheelchair. The changes were happening so fast, it was dizzying. Adding to the frustration of the situation was the fact that we had no idea what was causing this to happen. I struggled to lift my 6'4" son in and out of the car as we traveled from hospital to hospital to get brain scans, MRIs and a spinal tap, but nothing could explain the loss of mobility as my son became paralyzed from the waist down in a matter of weeks.

In desperation as his loss of mobility continued, I called frantically trying to find someone who could help us. I called the oncologists who had treated Nathan at Duke Medical Center. They looked at the test results and said there was nothing they could do; there was no evidence of another brain tumor. They hypothesized that it was something neurological. I told them we needed to be at Duke so that we could be under one roof with a team of physicians from different disciplines evaluating the tests to determine what was going on. I was adamant and I wasn't taking no for an answer. Finally, they agreed. We made the arrangements for a medical transport and flew to Duke.

When we arrived, the doctors told me they could not promise anything but they would do whatever they could to find the answer.

We were there eight days. Over that time specialists from every department examined, poked, prodded and ordered every test possible.

By the eighth day they found the answer. It was another brain tumor. This one was in the medulla, the center of the brain. It was an astrocytoma, a type of tumor that stretched its fingerlike tentacles through his brain. It was inoperable. It had been stealthily infiltrating Nathan's brain over the last couple of months and had not been detected in all the scans and MRIs until it was too late. As these eight days had passed, Nathan's mobility had decreased to the point that he was now completely paralyzed from his neck down. He was a quadriplegic.

It was Ash Wednesday. People around the hospital had ashes smudged on their foreheads. As any good Catholic knows, Ash Wednesday marks the beginning of Lent. The purpose of the ashes on the forehead is to remind us of our mortality. "From dust thou art and to dust thou shalt return."

Ironically, it was on Ash Wednesday when Nathan's oncologist walked into the room to tell him the findings of the tests. This oncologist had a son the same age as Nathan. He told Nathan that there was nothing more they could do. Nathan took the news stoically. He was composed as he thanked the doctor for his care and told him that he knew they had done everything they could for him. The doctor's eyes filled with tears as he accepted Nathan's thanks.

After the doctor walked out of the room, Nathan began to cry. The cry was like a loud mournful wail. As I stood there helplessly comforting him, he suddenly yelled out, "Riiiicky! Riiiicky!" I had no idea who he was calling for. There was no one by the name of Ricky in our family, and there was no one who had been caring for him who was named Ricky. I asked him, "Who are you calling for? Who is Ricky?"

In the mist of his wail he cried, "I sound...like... Lucille Ball!"

I couldn't believe it! Here he was literally on his deathbed and he was making jokes. In his mind he was able to look at the situation and listen to himself cry. He realized that as he cried out he sounded like the character Lucy of the show, I Love Lucy. He had watched those old shows in black-and-white on television years before and his loud cry reminded him of how the character Lucy would cry out for her husband Ricky whenever she was in trouble.

Nathan was looking Death in the eye and laughing.

* * *

Lesson 5: Laughter truly is the best medicine. Never take life too seriously.

CHAPTER 6

If it doesn't challenge you, it doesn't change you.

~ Fred Devito

The plan was to return home to die. The doctor told me that the paralysis was advancing at such a rate that he thought Nathan had 10 days to live.

As arrangements were made for Nathan to be put into hospice and make another flight by medical air transport, Nathan was coming to terms with his situation.

One of the nurses who had been caring for him walked into the room to give him some medication. He announced to her, "I'm dying."

"I know you are," she replied.

"I'll put in a good word for you when I see God," he said.

Suddenly, nurse after nurse began to visit the room. These were nurses we hadn't seen before. They were working with other patients and hadn't been involved in Nathan's care, but they seemed to appear hoping to receive Nathan's blessing. It made me smile to see Nathan's effect on people. They seemed amazed at his peace and acceptance of his situation. Once again, I was very proud of my sweet son.

From the very beginning of the original diagnosis almost three years earlier to the realization that death was around the corner, Nathan never complained. He was never angry. One time he did ask me why I thought cancer had happened to him. He wondered aloud what God's role was in his cancer. I told him, God didn't do this to him, He was helping us through it. I told him I thought that the cause was probably due to unknown environmental issues. As humans we had created a world filled with pollution and toxins and it was probably these toxins that had led to this tumor.

After we returned home, my greatest concern at this point was that Nathan not be afraid to die, therefore we talked about everything. Nathan was in the hospital bed that was set up in his bedroom. I slept in the same room in a bed close-by. We would talk late into the night. I loved those talks. I told him one night, "You know Nathan, you've won the lottery. You're getting out of here early. The rest of us are bumbling around trying to figure out the purpose of life. You've completed what you came to earth to do. In fact," I said, "I think you volunteered for this."

"What do you mean?" he asked.

"You have always liked challenges and I think you asked God for a challenge."

I explained, "I've come to believe in reincarnation. I think we come through this way multiple times. The way I imagine heaven is kind of like a basketball arena. God is on center court."

"I think the first time you cross over you get a seat in the peanut gallery, way up high. You can keep that seat if you want, or you can come back for another lifetime and try to live a good life, learn some soul lessons and get a better seat the next time you cross over. You can keep improving your seat in heaven's arena, life by life, until you reach God on center court."

"I think you asked for a challenge so you could make a big jump in your seat in that arena. I think you might be pretty close to center court. Over the last couple of years you have taught all of us so much about the important things in life. You have taught not only me and your dad and your sister Heather but you have taught your friends lessons that they will never forget."

* * *

Lesson 6: Your life situation will always have challenges. The goal of life is to be

present and try to find the lesson that the challenge is offering you.

CHAPTER 7

It is during our darkest moments that we must focus to see the light.
~ Aristotle Onassis.

Although the doctor had predicted that Nathan would die in 10 days, we were fortunate enough to have him 12 weeks. Each day was a blessing. Every morning the nurse from hospice would come to bathe Nathan. We would then lift him into the wheelchair and take him out onto the patio next to the pool. Mike, his dad, would fix him breakfast, his favorite meal. Mike would whip up different Jewish specialties, lox, eggs and onion, matzo brei or cheese blintzes. While the two men enjoyed breakfast together and talked about the mysteries of life, I would either go for a bike ride or go to yoga class.

Our days were filled with talking and listening to music. My brothers and sisters had sent gifts trying to lift his spirits including recordings of classic comedies. Nathan didn't really want to watch anything. He preferred to talk about what to expect when he crossed over.

Some of his questions were so innocent and some so funny, that they made me smile.

He asked, "How will I know where to go?"

"You just follow the light," I replied. "There will be a bright light and it will show you the way. It will be like the stars that the explorers used to follow as they crossed the ocean before compasses were invented. Just follow the light," I instructed.

"Granddad will also be there. You'll feel his hand squeeze your shoulder." My father had died a few years earlier. My dad had a trademark greeting when he walked into the room, he'd reach up and squeeze your shoulder to say hello.

"I'll finally get to meet Erik!" Nathan exclaimed. I had lost a baby at 5 months gestation when Nathan was a toddler. We had kept the memory of Erik alive as a way to talk about death with the kids. I had the miscarriage shortly before Christmas one year so a friend had given me a Christmas ornament that looked like a baby angel. Each year as we decorated the Christmas tree we would talk about Erik; how old he'd be that year, we'd imagine what he'd look like. By keeping his memory alive, the kids understood that they already knew someone in heaven.

Nathan had always liked having a girlfriend. His high school girlfriend had broken up with him when he was diagnosed with cancer. My heart ached for him when this happened but I understood that this was a big weight for the girlfriend to handle at this age. Still, he missed having the companionship and affection that only a girlfriend could offer.

During one of our late night talks Nathan asked me, "Are there any girls my age in heaven?"

The question made me smile. "Of course!" I replied. "Remember Helen Witty?" She was a girl about 2 years ahead of Nathan at school. Everyone knew Helen. She was one of the shining stars, top of her class and very involved in school. She had been roller-blading on a sidewalk and was hit and killed by another high school student who was under the influence of drugs and alcohol. The community was horrified at her death and her memory lived on. "Helen will be there and she'll introduce you to all her friends!" I reassured Nathan.

* * *

Lesson 7: When your child trusts you enough to ask a question, listen and answer to the best of your ability. Don't shy away from any issue or minimize the importance of their concern. I learned that I could be more resilient than I ever imagined and answer questions I never anticipated.

CHAPTER 8

*Very little is needed to make a happy life, it is
all within yourself, in your way of thinking.*
~ Marcus Aurelius

The ten days that the doctor expected Nathan
would live expanded to a total of 83 days. We knew
that each day was a blessing. Every night Mike and
I would lift Nathan into his chair and take him for
a walk around the block. It was nice to feel the evening breeze and look up to the stars but Nathan
was feeling the confinement. He wanted to go out
somewhere but of course we could not take him
in a regular car since he was completely paralyzed
from the neck down.

I called around to every car rental place in the

city and finally found one van that was equipped to transport people confined to wheelchairs. I rented it for two months. Now we could go places! We loaded Nathan into the van and set off for Monty's, an open-air restaurant on Biscayne Bay. They served great conch fritters there. As we strapped Nathan's chair into place in the back of the van, he exclaimed, "Put the pedal to the metal and let's get out of here!" He was so happy to feel a little bit of freedom.

* * *

Lesson 8: You make your own happiness. If you appreciate the little things in life, how can you not be happy when your heart is full of gratitude?

CHAPTER 9

We do not remember days, we remember moments.

~ Cesare Pavese

Nathan was four years older than his sister Heather. Heather idolized her big brother from the very start. If Nathan said something was cool, there was no question in Heather's mind, it was cool. The two of them would watch movies together at home when Mike and I would go out for the evening. When they were in high school we left them alone for the weekend a couple of times. They didn't have wild parties but they did have some funny escapades. Some of the stories first came to light when Heather was sharing memories of her brother at his memorial service.

As brother and sister, it was rare that they didn't get along, although Nathan knew how to tease Heather whenever he wanted to. But still, they turned to each other to talk about important things in a teenager's life. Heather asked him advice about guys at school and Nathan shared his girlfriend problems with her.

One day when Nathan was on hospice, Heather crawled into bed next to him. She took his paralyzed arm and draped it over her shoulder so that he was hugging her.

She cried in his arms and asked, "How am I going to make it on my own without you? I need you to help me deal with Mom and Dad."

"Don't worry," he reassured her, "We'll see each other again in the blink of an eye. I'm just going ahead to open the door for you."

Later that night, I sat on Nathan's bed and we talked. "You know, as Heather's older brother I expect you to keep an eye on her when you get to the other side."

"Don't worry," he promised, "I will."

I cannot begin to tell you what a comfort that has been over the years as Heather traveled to the faraway places of Singapore, Bhutan and Vietnam. I may have worried, but my worry was tempered by the reassurance that Nathan had her back.

One morning shortly after breakfast, Nathan was in resting in his bed in his room when suddenly he had a seizure. He had experienced only a couple of seizures in the past and none had left a lasting effect. This seizure was different. This seizure left Nathan with aphasia, the loss of the ability to speak.

I realized what had happened immediately. I didn't want Nathan to be scared or stressed. I calmly explained that we would still be able to communicate. He would blink his eyes once for yes and twice for no. We were communicating that way for a few minutes when suddenly for some miraculous reason he regained the ability to speak!

The first words he said were, "I was so worried I wouldn't be able to tell you how much I love you!" Then it was my turn to be speechless, my eyes filled with tears and my heart overflowed with love. This was a moment I would never forget.

* * *

Lesson 9: Don't take tomorrow for granted. Don't wait to tell someone that you love them.

CHAPTER 10

A real friend is one who walks in when the rest of the world walks out.

~ Walter Winchell

Our talks in the evenings continued. My dad had died several years earlier and Nathan and Heather had attended the funeral. Following the funeral service we had a celebration of my dad's life. My father was Irish so we played Irish music, served corned beef sandwiches, beer and Irish whiskey.

"After you cross over," I began, "We will want to celebrate your life. We want to serve you favorite food. What would you like us to serve?"

Breakfast, had always been Nathan's favorite

meal so he gave a long list of his favorite dishes. "Bagels and lox, omelets, blintzes, mimosas and...a ham...for you." He loved the Jewish breakfasts that his dad fixed for him each morning but he wanted to acknowledge the Gentile side of his genetic makeup by including a ham on the menu.

"How will my friends know about the reception?" he asked.

"When you die, I will call a couple of your friends and they will call the others to let them know. Plus, we will have an obituary in the newspaper which will explain when the service will be and the reception will be held immediately after the service. Anyone who comes to the service will be invited to the reception.'

"Can you do me a favor?" he asked. "At the end of the obituary can you write in bold letters, FREE FOOD? Then I know my friends will come."

"I don't think you need to worry, they'll be there." I reassured him with confidence; I knew his friends would be at the funeral service.

Nathan had about a dozen good friends who came by on a regular basis during the last weeks of his life. It was interesting to me to see the character of his friends. They didn't shy away when they saw Nathan lying paralyzed in his bed. He was thin, his face gaunt; he looked like death. In my experience often adults feel uncomfortable around death and often stay away because they don't know what to say or how to act in the presence of a dying person.

One morning his group of friends entered his room sitting on the chairs and leaning against the bookcases. They came to lift Nathan's spirits. They talked about school, their classes, sports and recent episodes of their favorite TV shows. As I walked past the doorway of his room I heard Nathan say to the group, "I'm dying." Those two words broke the bravado of these strong young men. I heard the whole group begin to cry, one by one. I was so touched. A group of strong, vital young men with their whole life before them saw their own mortality as one of their group prepared for the end of life. I was so proud and touched that these tough guys could display their emotions in front of each other.

* * *

Lesson 10: Don't disappear when a friend or loved one is facing death. You don't need to worry about not knowing what to say. The dying and their families do not want your words of wisdom, they simply need your presence and support.

CHAPTER 11

For life and death are one, even as the river and the sea are one.

~ Khalil Gibran

"After you die," I continued one night as I sat on the end of his bed. "Would you like to be buried or cremated?" My dad had been cremated and we had a family gathering where we had scattered his ashes along with flowers in the St Johns River in north Florida.

"I want to be cremated," Nathan replied.

"Where would you like your ashes scattered?"

"At Iceberg Lake."

Iceberg Lake was the beautiful spot in Glacier

National Park where this journey began almost 3 years earlier. It was the place so beautiful that I had said God lived there. Nathan felt the same way. It was where he would find his final resting place.

During those days, meditation was the tool that gave me the inner strength that I needed. My meditation became part of my spiritual practice. When I meditated I felt as though I was sitting in a room with God and I never felt closer to Him than during those days when I was caring for my son. God truly was holding me up and helping me every step of the way.

One day during this period of time on hospice, both Nathan and I meditated together. When I was done, I opened my eyes and looked at Nathan. By this point he was very pale, his eyes sunk into his head and he looked like the picture of death. But as I looked at him as he continued to meditate I noticed that his face looked radiant. When he opened his eyes, I asked him if anything different had happened during his meditation.

"Yes," he told me, "I saw the other side!"

"What was it like?" I asked.

"I can't put it into words, but it was so beautiful!" My heart leapt with joy. Nathan was anxious about what to expect as death was coming closer. God gave him a preview to assuage his worries and concerns.

One day led to the next as we sat with Nathan in God's waiting room. We appreciated every moment and developed a rhythm to our day as the predicted 10 days grew to over 80. As every day passed I talked to God and told Him how I thought the process should go. I had lots of thoughts and opinions and offered God plenty of unsolicited advice. One day it suddenly occurred to me that God did not need a micro-manager. He had handled plenty of deaths before and He had a lot more experience than I did with it. With that realization, as silly as it seems, I felt as if the weight of the world was lifted off my shoulders. I told God I trusted that He had this situation under control. When I surrendered being a helicopter mother and allowed God to take over, I felt a tremendous feeling of peace. I knew everything would be alright.

It was two days after that concession that things changed. The morning started off as a normal routine. The hospice nurse arrived and bathed Nathan. I went to yoga class and Mike fixed Nathan's breakfast and fed him outside his room, on the patio by the pool.

When I returned from yoga I walked out to the patio and found Nathan in his wheelchair panting so quickly that he could barely speak.

"What's wrong, Nathan?" I asked.

"Death of a loved one" he replied. Changes had been taking place in his brain over the last few weeks. His thoughts and his words did not always correspond, but I knew what he meant. He was dying.

The paralysis was reaching his lungs. It took all of his energy to breathe and he could no longer speak. We had no way of knowing how much longer he had but we knew the time was drawing near. It was Friday morning. As the evening fell I told Heather and Mike that we would take turns sitting up with Nathan during the night. I had been sleeping in the room with him while he was on hospice but I wanted someone to be awake with him at all times. I did not want him to be alone during this time. I did not want him to die alone. We rotated our shifts Friday, Saturday and Sunday. On Monday afternoon two of his best friends came by to see him. I was glad that they came by but I was anxious for them to leave, I didn't want to share the remaining time with anyone outside of our family.

It was about 4:30 in the afternoon. As I sat at the end of Nathan's bed, I suddenly saw a cone of light coming from the top of his head. It was a little off to the side and angled up toward the ceiling. There was no light source in the ceiling and no lamp nearby. The only windows were on the opposite side of the room. I saw the light and I couldn't figure out where it was coming from. I put my hand through the light and realized it was coming from Nathan's body. "Nathan, you are getting ready to leave us," I said. The light remained for five to ten minutes. Shortly after that it disappeared and Nathan's breathing reverted from the staccato panting to a regular rhythmic breathing. I called Heather into the room. "Heather, come quickly, something is happening!" Nathan took one more breath and he was gone.

* * *

Lesson 11: It is a sacred gift to be with a loved one as they cross over. It can be hard to let them go but if we truly love them, how can we ask them to stay when relief is just a heartbeat away?

Heather, Peggy and Michael Gaines scattering Nathan's ashes in a mountain lake at Glacier N.P.

CHAPTER 12

Death – the last sleep?
No, It is the final awakening.
~ Walter Scott

Death is the sacred bookend to Birth. There is a distinct parallel between coming into this world and leaving this world. As a Labor and Delivery room nurse I had helped many women bring babies into the world. With both birth and death, there is pain and trepidation, fear of the unknown. But both passages lead to new Life.

When the time came for Nathan to cross over, I was very sad but I was not depressed. I had never felt angry or alone during the ordeal; I knew we were supported by something bigger than ourselves every step of the way. Instead of thinking that this was the worst thing that could ever happen to our family, I thought, "I am so grateful Nathan was part of our life for 20 years. I'm so grateful that I got to be his mother."

There isn't a day that goes by that I don't think of my son. I honestly feel that I was chosen to go through that experience so that I could share with others the important practice of meditation. Meditation is a life skill that everyone needs to know.

* * *

Lesson 12: It is our most difficult experiences that offer us the greatest spiritual growth.

CHAPTER 13

The Practice of Meditation

I knew I had been given the gift of a tool that everyone needed to know about.

Everyone has events in their life that can seem to be too difficult to handle. It may be an overwhelming number of little things that add up, until you just cannot take it anymore or it may be one crushing blow that stops you in your tracks. Whatever it is, you can handle it when you have the peace and inner strength that you find when you take time to be still and meditate.

As a society, we have become consumed with

the external worries and trappings of life. We are always connected to something or someone else with our cell phone and computer. Our eyes are constantly focused downward as we check the texts, apps, and contacts from sites and people we may have little real connection with. Meanwhile, the true essence of life is passing us by. We don't look up long enough to notice the sky; we have no idea if the day is sunny or cloudy. We only notice the weather when it interferes with our comfort. As we walk to our car with our head scanning our IPhone, we miss the cool breeze that brushes our cheek. We can't remember the last time we heard a bird singing or noticed the phase of the moon. When was the last time that we looked up at the night sky, simply to admire the stars? Instead of noticing the gifts the universe is giving us, we focus on our never-ending list of things to do. We ruminate about yesterday and worry about tomorrow, all while forgetting to live today.

We've lost our soul, our true connection with ourselves. We feel alone, unsupported by the universe. It's you and me against the world. And conventional wisdom tells us the world is a scary place. Therefore, you feel as though you always need to be on-guard, always on alert. You live in a constant state of fight or flight, ready to defend yourself or run for cover at a moment's notice. No wonder we feel panicked. We believe the world is out of control.

The truth is, life is unpredictable and sometimes incredibly tough to handle, but the universe has not abandoned you. We are not on our own.

With meditation you learn to find calm and inner strength. You feel a true connection with the Source. You know that no matter how difficult life may become, you will have the inner peace that comes from a peace not of this world. It is a knowing that you are loved and supported by something greater than yourself and you are never alone.

One way to find that inner peace, the inner calm and stillness that's missing from our life, is with meditation.

Is there Proof Meditation Works?

People have been meditating more than 3000 years in the East but it's fairly new to the Western world. In the early 1970s, Herbert Benson a Harvard physician began studying stress related illnesses and noted that it seemed to be a phenomenon of the west.[1] When they looked at the East, in countries such as India, with its stressful environment of poverty and overcrowding, they found that the population did not have the same health problems. Researchers hypothesized that it was due to the prevalence of meditation.

Now, 45 years later there is a plethora of studies showing that meditation actually changes the brain. A group of Harvard affiliated researchers at Massachusetts General Hospital found that within 8 weeks of meditative practice, there was measurable change in the amygdala or fight and flight center of the brain.[2]

With meditation, you will still worry and still lose your temper but the way that you look at things will begin to change. I realized that is what happened to me with my son. I was able to look at life differently. When I looked at the situation instead of feeling that my son's death was the worst thing that could ever have happened, I thought I was so glad that Nathan had been part of our family for 20 years. I was so grateful I had been chosen to be his mother. Instead of focusing on what we had lost, I focused on the gift we had been given. I was able to do this because my brain had changed and so had my perspective on life.

How Does Meditation Work?

When we are stressed we go into the fight and flight state. In this state, our breathing is shallow, our heart rate increases and our blood pressure goes up.

The fight and flight state is a protective response that was helpful when we were cave men and were being chased by saber-toothed tigers. While we were escaping, we were in the fight and flight state but once we got away from the tiger we were able to relax. Our heart rate slowed down, our breathing became deeper and our blood pressure returned to normal.

The problem is, today we LIVE in a fight and flight state. We've forgotten how to return to the relaxed state. We live in a continual state of alertness. "What's that sound? What's going on? I've got to remember this; I can't forget that!"

That's the way we live, but our bodies weren't created to live constantly in this state so as a result, we begin to manifest signs of stress. We begin having headaches, neck and back pain; grind our teeth at night, have trouble sleeping, suffer from indigestion, and high blood pressure. Our tempers are short, we stress eat, drink and numb our feelings with medication.

This constant level of stress is killing us. But we can do something about it.

The Magic Key

The magic key to relieving the stress and getting out of the fight and flight state is becoming aware of our breath. When we are in the fight and flight state we breathe shallow; we only use the top part of our lungs. But our lungs go to the bottom of our rib cage. We are designed to breathe with our full lungs; that's why they are there.

Why this Works

As you probably remember from high school biology, the diaphragm is a dome shaped muscle that separates our lungs from our abdominal cavity. When we breathe shallow (which is what we do in the fight and flight state) the diaphragm just sits there, nothing happens. But when we breathe with our full lungs, the full lungs put pressure on the dome shaped diaphragm causing the diaphragm to flatten out. When we exhale, the diaphragm returns to its dome shape; when we inhale it flattens out again. This is significant because there is a nerve that innervates the diaphragm, called the vagus nerve. When the diaphragm moves up and down with our breath, the vagus nerve is stimulated and it sends the message to the brain to relax.

Breathing with our full lungs, diaphragmatically, is the way we are supposed to be breathing all the time but right now we are mindful of the way we are breathing only while we meditate. As we become more mindful of the way we are breathing, diaphragmatic breathing will become a habit and eventually we will breathe this way all the time not just when we are meditating.

Try this exercise

Sit up straight, with your head, neck and spine in alignment. Put your feet flat on the floor. Place your hands on your ribcage. As you breathe in through your nostrils, breathe just a little deeper than you normally breathe. Don't breathe as though you are trying to blow up a balloon. Breathe as though you are breathing in the fragrance of a beautiful flower. Feel your ribs expand as you breathe in. Notice how your ribs contract as you exhale. Breathe in again and feel your ribs expand; feel your ribs contract as you exhale.

Now put your hands in your lap. Allow your eyes to close and relax your shoulders. Breathe in again and be mindful of your ribs expanding as you inhale and contract as you exhale. Continue breathing in and breathing out.

As you breathe in take your awareness to the tip of your nose. Notice the cool air as you breathe in and your ribs expand. Notice how the air is warm as you exhale and your ribs contract.

You can think to yourself: "I am breathing in; I am breathing out. Cool air in; warm air out. I am breathing in; I am breathing out." This is a brief meditation. Try it for 2 minutes and then notice how you feel. You will find that you are feeling calmer, more relaxed and focused.

Myths about meditation

As a nurse, I get referrals from cardiologists, internists and psychologists to teach their patients meditation. When people come to me for instruction, the most common statement is "I can't meditate, I have too many thoughts."

The fact is, everybody has too many thoughts. Everybody is bouncing from one thought to the next. But research has found that a wandering mind is often an unhappier mind because often our mind focuses on worries and concerns.[3]

There are many myths about meditation. A couple of the myths include the mistaken idea that meditation is about mind control or that meditation is about stopping your thoughts or blanking out your mind. All of these ideas are wrong.

It's impossible to stop your mind from thinking and meditation has no intention of doing such a thing. Meditation is exercise for your brain. When you are meditating and your thoughts wander, simply bring your awareness back to your breath. Every time your mind wanders, just notice it and bring your awareness back to your breath. This action of noticing that your mind has wandered and refocusing your awareness on your breath is like a bicep curl for your brain. As your mind wanders off and you guide it gently back to your breath, you are actually training your brain to stay focused and on task. Researchers have found when distracted, the person who meditates is able to refocus faster than the person who doesn't meditate.[4]

If you feel that you would like to experience the power and benefits of meditation, Peggy can be contacted through her website: www.MeditationWithPeggyGaines.com

1 *The Relaxation Response*, Herbert Benson, MD
   Harper tech 1975

2 http://blogs.scientificamerican.com/guest-blog/
   what-does-mindfulness-meditation-do-to-
   your-brain/

3 http://greatergood.berkeley.edu/article/item/
   how_to_focus_a_wandering_mind

4 http://lifehacker.com/what-happens-to-the-
   brain-when-you-meditate-and-how-it-

ABOUT THE AUTHOR

 Peggy Gaines, RN, BSN is a nurse educator and is nationally board certified as a Clinical Meditation Specialist. She has been meditating more than 18 years and has been teaching meditation over 6 years. She is married and the mother of two children, Nathan and Heather. When their son Nathan was 17 year old, he developed a malignant brain tumor. Peggy relied on meditation to help her stay calm and focused as she and her husband navigated the care for their son.

Everyone has some type of stress to deal with in life, and everyone can benefit from knowing skills and techniques that can be used when life gets tough. Meditation is such a tool.

Peggy teaches meditation classes for individuals and businesses to cope with the demands and pressures of life. She lives in Coconut Grove, Florida with Michael, her husband of 31 years.